Adventure Book For Boys: Super Fun Things To Do

Speedy Publishing LLC
40 E. Main St. #1156
Newark, DE 19711

www.speedypublishing.com

9781681275475
First Printed January 5, 2015

Football is the most popular sport in the world. Over one billion fans watch World Cup Football on television.

HOME
GUEST
53
15

More than 38 million Americans hunt and fish.

21
11

13
18
24
23

About 3 million people camp at parks run by the National Park Service every year according to the Outdoor Industry Association.

The first "hoops" were actually just peach baskets and the first backboards were made of wire.

Indoor bowling lanes made their debut in 1840 in New York City.

A dojo can be any place where you can learn karate.

In the early 1980s, mostly only teenagers were riding snowboards. Because most major ski resorts catered to older crowds, snowboards were decidedly unpopular on the slopes. It wasn't until 1983-84 that the first major ski resort opened its slopes to snowboarders.

Did you know the number of possible ways of playing the first four moves for both sides in a game of chess is 318,979,564,000?

Did you know that skiing was originally a form of transportation in the mountains of Europe, well before it became a sport?

The Piano was invented in 1698 by an Italian, Bartolomeo Cristofori. There are over 12,000 parts in a piano, 10,000 which are moving.

Bicycles are used for transport, recreation, competitive racing, courier delivery and a range of other tasks.

The windiest surf city in the world is Wellington, capital of New Zealand. The highest tides in the world can be found in Canada, at the Bay of Fundy. Sometimes the difference between high and low tide is 16.3 meters (53.5 feet).

The guitar is a stringed instrument that makes music from the vibrations of strings. It's also a fretted and plucked string instrument. Fretted means that it has frets, or metal wires, on the finger board to help play the notes.

In fact, gloves were introduced into boxing not for safety reasons, but to increase hits to the head and dramatic knockouts.

Paintball is a game developed in the 1980s that soon became popular worldwide. Players shoot pellets of paint from airguns at opposing players in a strategic game similar to the children's classic Capture the Flag.

Badminton is the Fastest racket sport with shuttle clocking speed in excess of 200 mph.

Prior to the use of rackets in tennis, people used their palms to hit the ball back and forth. The palm method was replaced in the 1500s when rackets were introduced. The word tennis evolved from the French term 'tenez'. The modern game became much more structured in the 1800s, and the first Wimbledon Championships were played in 1877 in London, England.

Video games can be played on a number of different platforms. This includes game consoles, handheld systems, computers, mobile phones, and others.

69
SINCE
W

Drums are an essential in most kinds of music from military bands to rock and pop.

Kite flying was banned in China during the Cultural Revolution. Anyone found flying a kite was sent to jail for up to three years and their kites destroyed. The Chinese name for a kite is Fen Zheng, which means wind harp.

www.ingramcontent.com/pod-product-compliance
Lightning Source LLC
LaVergne TN
LVHW060829170826
845678LV00010B/1937

* 9 7 9 8 8 6 9 4 5 7 3 0 1 *